# Risking It All

# Program Consultants

**Stephanie Abraham Hirsh, Ph.D.**
Associate Director
National Staff Development Council
Dallas, Texas

**Louise Matteoni, Ph.D.**
Professor of Education
Brooklyn College
City University of New York

**Karen Tindel Wiggins**
Social Studies Consultant
Richardson Independent School District
Richardson, Texas

**Renee Levitt**
Educational Consultant
Scarsdale, New York

**Steck-Vaughn Company**

A Subsidiary of National Education Corporation

# Risking It All

### BY
## Melissa Stone

# Steck-Vaughn Literature Library
## Moments in American History

RISKING IT ALL
REBELLION'S SONG
CREATIVE DAYS
RACING TO THE WEST
YOU DON'T OWN ME!
CLOUDS OF WAR
A CRY FOR ACTION
LARGER THAN LIFE
FLYING HIGH
BRIGHTER TOMORROWS

**Illustrations:** Bradley Clark: 8-9, 11, 13, 14-15, 16-17, 19; Arvis Stewart: cover art, 20-21, 22-23, 25, 26, 27, 28-29, 31; Rae Ecklund: 32-33, 34-35, 36, 39, 40, 43; Linda Graves: 44-45, 46, 48, 50-51, 53, 54, 55; Ron Himler: 56-57, 58, 61, 62, 65, 67; Lyle Miller: 68-69, 70, 73, 75, 76, 77, 79.

**Project Editor:** Anne Souby

**Design:** Kirchoff/Wohlberg, Inc.

ISBN 0-8114-4075-3

# CONTENTS

# 1600

**AMERIGO VESPUCCI**
The Old World first discovers
the New World.
(1493-1507)

**HENRY HUDSON**
Finding a Northwest
Passage mattered mo
to him than life itself.
(1610)

**POCAHONTAS**
She looked at the
white man and
saw a friend.
(1607)

**ANNE BRADSTREET** ▼
She proved that a
woman could have
two careers.
(1630-1650)

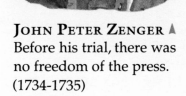

**JOHN PETER ZENGER** ▲
Before his trial, there was
no freedom of the press.
(1734-1735)

**KING PHILIP** ►
He fought to restore
power and honor to
his tribe.
(1675-1676)

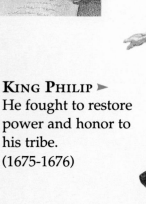

# AMERIGO VESPUCCI

## A CURIOUS MERCHANT

Today, Christopher Columbus begins his incredible voyage. He will sail due west from Spain across the great ocean. Crowds surround him at seaside. He has promised to bring back spices and perfumes and jewels.

Columbus smiles as he looks up at his great ship, the *Santa Maria*. Then he looks over at me, his friend, Amerigo Vespucci.

"It will be a long journey," he says. "Wish me luck."

**D**ID you hear the news?" cried Giovanni Vespucci as he burst into his uncle's office in March 1493. "Christopher Columbus has returned! He has returned from his voyage across the Sea of Darkness!"

"What did he say? Did he find Asia in the western part of the great ocean?" asked Amerigo Vespucci.

"Yes," shouted Giovanni. "Columbus says Asia is only 3,000 miles west of here! That is not as far away as you calculated, Uncle."

Amerigo frowned. "Columbus cannot be right," he said. "Most learned men have agreed that the world is more than 22,000 miles around. If Asia is only 3,000 miles from here, then the world is much smaller than scholars have predicted."

"Well, Uncle, that is what Columbus is reporting," replied Giovanni with a shrug.

Amerigo leaned back in his chair and stared through the window at the sky. "Is it possible?" he asked himself. "Could so many people have been wrong? Could the earth be so much smaller?"

Following work that night, Amerigo rushed home. He wanted to study this problem more. He lit the candles and began to pore over his notes and scientific papers.

For months Amerigo tinkered with calculations.

At night he studied the changes in the stars and the moon. He believed that the answer to his quest lay in the sky. By tracking the changes in the moon, he felt, he would be able to predict distances on earth that had not yet been measured. Finally, he came to a turning point in his research.

"Columbus did not find Asia," he declared to Giovanni. "Asia cannot lie 3,000 miles to the west."

"Perhaps Columbus misjudged the distance he traveled," suggested his nephew. "Or maybe the earth is really smaller than we believe it to be."

Amerigo paused. "Perhaps," he said slowly. "All I know is that if I were younger and a little richer, I would sail across the ocean and prove my theory."

F OR the next six years, Amerigo tried to concentrate on his growing mercantile business. However, reports of Christopher Columbus's second and third voyages made him even more restless and determined to prove his own ideas.

One night Amerigo came to a drastic decision. "I have to go to sea," he thought. "I have to prove to the world that the early scholars were not wrong and that the earth is as big as we believe it to be. I must find out if Columbus has really reached the shores of Asia."

By the spring of 1499, all the arrangements had been made for financing the journey. Amerigo had outfitted six ships and hired a reliable crew. On the voyage, Amerigo would chart the ships' course. Juan de la Cosa, who had sailed with Columbus twice, would be the chief pilot.

"I can't believe it," Amerigo whispered to himself. "I'm going to do it. I'm really going to sail across the ocean."

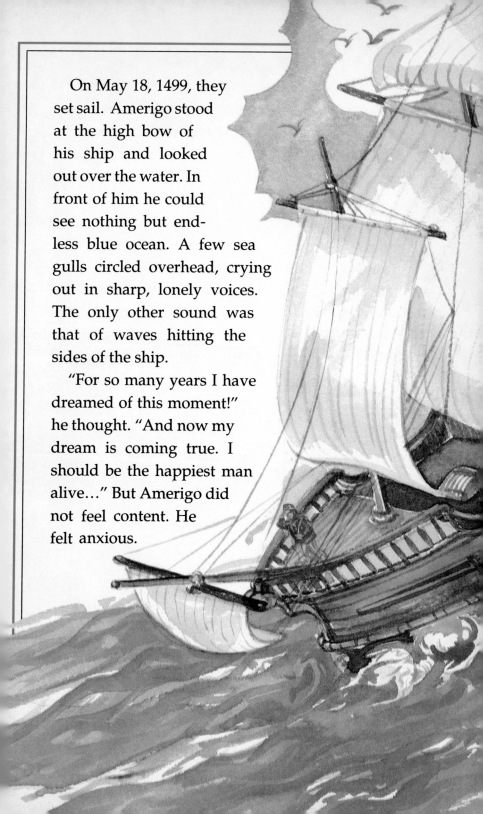

On May 18, 1499, they set sail. Amerigo stood at the high bow of his ship and looked out over the water. In front of him he could see nothing but endless blue ocean. A few sea gulls circled overhead, crying out in sharp, lonely voices. The only other sound was that of waves hitting the sides of the ship.

"For so many years I have dreamed of this moment!" he thought. "And now my dream is coming true. I should be the happiest man alive…" But Amerigo did not feel content. He felt anxious.

The vastness of the ocean overwhelmed him. He became concerned about possible dangers that could interrupt the journey. What if the ships ran into a storm? What if they drifted off course and never found land? What would they find on this journey?

At that moment, Juan de la Cosa walked up to him. "If you will be up all night charting the stars, I suggest you rest now."

Amerigo thanked the pilot for his concern. He decided that the rest would help him put aside his doubts and give him the energy he needed to face whatever lay ahead. He grabbed a blanket and found a corner sheltered from the wind. This was the best type of sleeping arrangement the ship had to offer.

Soon the rhythm of the ship lulled him to sleep. Yet, before drifting off, he had one last thought.

"When I return to Spain, I shall be considered a hero or a fraud. Others will not know of the vast energy I have invested in this journey. They will only want to know what I am able to prove. I wonder whether I will be right or wrong."

A few days later, Amerigo's small fleet reached the Canary Islands off the northwest coast of Africa. Here they stopped for supplies of fresh water, firewood, and extra food. Then they swung westward and sailed across the open ocean.

FOR 24 days Amerigo and his crew saw nothing but water. They lived on salted beef and pork, beans, chickpeas, and biscuits. When the fresh water ran out, they drank wine. The rough seas disturbed their sleep. Worms dug holes through the ships' hulls, causing many leaks.

Juan de la Cosa assigned men to pump out the water. But when violent storms battered the ships, every inch was drenched in spite of all efforts.

Amerigo tried to keep up the men's spirits. He knew the voyage was much less romantic than many had dreamed. He stayed busy with his studies. Every night he plotted the position of the moon and the stars. He longed for the moment when the sailors would find land, and he could determine the actual distance they had traveled.

AT last, after many days at sea, the lookout on Amerigo's ship gave a joyful shout.

"Land, ho!"

Amerigo felt his heart pounding as he ran to the bow and scanned the horizon. Was it true? Had they reached land? As Amerigo looked, he sighted a faint rise of land. He did not know it at the time, but he and his men were the first Europeans ever to see the land now known as Brazil.

Juan de la Cosa lowered a rowboat. Amerigo and several other men climbed into it. Rowing furiously, they soon reached the shore.

The men were amazed at the surroundings they encountered. The thick jungle grew down to the water. Nowhere could the men land and go ashore.

"Look at these trees!" shouted several.

"How will we ever be able to pass through here?" quizzed others.

The men had never before seen anything like this. One man questioned, "Where are Asia's marble-bridged cities and great stores of riches?"

When they returned to the ship, Amerigo was almost ready to proclaim that this was not Asia. According to his calculations, they had not traveled far enough to reach the Far East. Instead he waited. "Let's travel down the coast," he said to Juan de la Cosa. "Travelers report that there is a big city on the eastern coast of Asia."

Amerigo and his ships traveled 1,000 miles down the coastline. At each stop they found more jungles and a few native people. Nothing they saw fit the descriptions of Asia.

"You see!" exclaimed Amerigo triumphantly. "This isn't Asia at all. I believe we have discovered a new continent!"

Finally, the ships sailed for home. Amerigo could not wait to share the results of the expedition. The men were overcome with thoughts of their own discovery. "Just think," said one sailor. "While we have lived our lives on one side of the ocean, other people have been living very different lives on the other side."

Everyone in Europe was stunned by Amerigo's discovery. He even received support to make a second journey to confirm his findings.

A MERIGO Vespucci never became as famous as Christopher Columbus. But in 1507, a German mapmaker decided to honor Amerigo. On his map of the New World, he labeled the new lands "America." Today our continent still bears the name of this inquisitive Italian merchant and explorer.

# HENRY HUDSON
## THE LAST VOYAGE

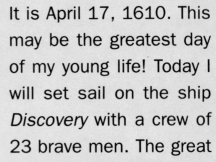

It is April 17, 1610. This may be the greatest day of my young life! Today I will set sail on the ship *Discovery* with a crew of 23 brave men. The great explorer, Henry Hudson, is our captain. We will sail up the coast until we find the Northwest Passage—a new waterway to China. All of us are hoping for calm waters and strong winds.

But, of course, nothing is certain. The sea is mysterious…

T HE men on board the ship *Discovery* were beginning to panic. Each day the weather turned colder. Each night the darkness lasted longer. Clearly winter was approaching. Yet Henry Hudson, the ship's captain, showed no signs of turning back. Day after day he led his crew deeper into strange waters.

Henry Greene, a young sailor, shivered as he gazed at the water. How much longer would Captain Hudson continue this search? Finally he gathered up his courage and approached the captain's door.

"Captain Hudson?" he asked, timidly knocking at the closed door.

"Enter." Hudson's loud, confident voice boomed back at him. The captain's log book was open to the date — October 25, 1610.

Henry Greene slipped into the cabin. "I just thought you should know, sir, that I've seen ice forming in the water of the bay. Perhaps, well—perhaps now would be a good time to set sail for England before the journey becomes impossible."

"Come, come, Greene," Hudson said, walking over to pat the young sailor's arm. "I am the captain of this ship. I know what I'm doing. I came to find a passageway to China. And I won't turn back until I've found it!"

"But we've been in this bay almost seven weeks, sir, and winter is closing in fast! The bay is filling with ice. The boat will not be able to move."

"Look, Greene," barked Captain Hudson. "I like you. Next to my son, you're probably my favorite crew member. But don't question my judgment. Put your trust in me and my experience, and do as I say."

"Yes, sir," said young Greene. He left Captain Hudson's cabin and returned to his post. He wanted to put his faith in his captain. But in his heart, he feared that Captain Hudson's plan would lead to disaster.

A week later, Captain Hudson called his crew together.

"Men," he said, "we will set up camp on the shore of the bay and prepare for winter. I can't guarantee safe passage to England until the spring. The ice is moving in too quickly for us to reach open water."

"We'll never survive the winter here, Captain Hudson!" shouted one of the crew members.

"You're to blame for not turning back," yelled another.

"That's right!" cried the other sailors.

Henry Greene did not speak. He simply stood, frozen with fear, near the bow of the ship. His mind was racing. Could they last an entire winter in this wilderness? Would they find enough food to eat? Would they freeze to death?

The men were still grumbling as they went ashore and began setting up camp. They knew they were in for a long, hard winter. But no one was prepared for the severe conditions that developed. Before long, the weather grew bitter. Temperatures stayed below freezing. Strong winds made it seem even colder. Many of the men suffered frostbite and became lame. By the end of November, one man had died and several others were sick.

As Henry Greene had feared, lack of food also became a problem. The *Discovery* did not have enough to last the winter. Captain Hudson sent men out to hunt, but they brought back only a few wild birds. As expected, the supply of bread, meal, peas, pork, and butter was disappearing rapidly. The men began to feel hunger gnawing at their stomachs.

WHEN Captain Hudson announced that he would ration the food, the men became even more distressed. They began fighting among themselves. They hurled insults at each other. Most of all, they burned with rage and blamed Captain Hudson for their situation.

"It isn't all the captain's fault," Henry Greene told a fellow crewman one icy January day. "He's trying to make sure we all survive."

"Well, of course you'd say that," laughed the seaman bitterly. "He treats his son and you better than the rest of us. He gives you both the easiest chores to do. He doubles your rations. Then, you have the nerve to pretend you don't even know it."

"What are you talking about?" stammered Greeene.

"See what I mean?" snapped the seaman. "You may think we don't notice, but we're not blind. Oh, no, my friend, we're not blind!"

With that, the seaman turned and stormed away. But his words lingered in Henry Greene's head. Could it be true?

Greene knew he had never asked for special treatment from the captain. He was hurt that the other crew members were talking about him. He decided to watch the captain to see if the seaman was right.

That night at supper he watched closely as Captain Hudson parceled out the food. Each man got a crust of bread, a small strip of dried pork, and half a cup of thin broth.

When Greene's turn came, however, Hudson cut off a large piece of bread and scooped up a full cup of broth. He also chose a particularly large strip of pork to drop onto Greene's plate.

Greene could feel the eyes of the other crew members staring at him hatefully. His face burned with embarrassment. He was shocked to realize that his fellow crewmen were right. The captain was not a fair and just leader.

Several days later, Greene witnessed another shocking scene. For no apparent reason, the captain flew into a rage. He accused Richard Whitely, the ship's cook, of stealing food. He demanded to search the man's sea chest.

It was too much for Greene to bear. The cook was kind and honest and would have given up his life for any of his crewmates. It made Greene furious to see Whitely treated so unjustly.

Suddenly the captain turned toward the frightened cook and shouted, "If you don't open your sea chest right now, I shall have you hanged!"

When Captain Hudson threatened to hang Whitely, Henry's blood ran cold. He began to hate this man who was so cruel to his own crew. Fear and hunger increased his anger toward the leader who had brought them to this condition. "I'll get even with you, you tyrant!" Greene vowed to himself.

For the next several months, Greene did not act on his feelings. He needed all his energy just to stay alive. But he never forgot his vow to get revenge.

B Y early June, the ice in the bay had melted. At last the *Discovery* could set sail. The men were overjoyed at the thought of going home.

But one evening Greene heard Captain Hudson talking to his son John.

John asked, "Father, how long will it take us to sail to England?"

Captain Hudson replied, "We're not going home yet, son. I will not return to England a failure!"

Henry Greene's mouth dropped open in shock. He couldn't believe what he had just heard. How could the captain continue to risk the lives of the crew members to save his own reputation? Greene was determined not to let the captain carry through his plan and lead them into further disaster.

Greene began holding secret meetings with the crew members. He urged them to mutiny. He wanted them to rebel against Captain Hudson and take over the ship's command.

By June 21, the men had agreed to Greene's idea. They were ready to mutiny. That night they gathered to make their final plans.

"All right," said Greene. "If Captain Hudson loves this bay so much, let him stay here. We can set him adrift in the rowboat and let him fend for himself. Here's what we'll do. We'll grab him and tie him up today!"

"And his son, too!" cried one of the seamen.

"That's right," said Greene. "Both of them can rot in these waters!"

"That's fine," spoke up the ship's carpenter. "But consider this. There isn't enough food for us all to make it back to England. I say we send the sick men with Hudson and his son. Then we'll have seven fewer mouths to feed on our journey."

Greene paused. No one spoke up to argue with the carpenter. Greene knew it was wrong to cast men adrift because they were sick. But he also knew the carpenter was right. They would never be able to complete their voyage with so many sick people on board and so many mouths to feed. He hated the action he knew he would have to take.

"All right," said Greene finally. "It's settled."

THE next morning, Greene and his men waited outside the captain's cabin. When Captain Hudson opened his door, the men grabbed him and tied his arms behind his back. Then they found Hudson's son, John, and threw him and his father into the rowboat. Finally, they rounded up the seven sick men and put them into the open boat, too.

Quickly Greene and his men lowered the boat into the water. Then Greene gave the order to open the sails, and the *Discovery* moved toward home. Greene tried not to look back. But he couldn't help himself. He stole one quick glance over his shoulder, and his heart sank.

A tiny rowboat bobbed rhythmically in the water. Eight men stared at him, weary and weeping and calling out for pity. They could not believe that their friends—men who had lived, eaten, and worked with them—could abandon them. Their eyes and hands begged for mercy.

But Captain Hudson sat still and silent. His eyes pierced Greene to his very soul. And that look would haunt Greene for the rest of his life.

# POCAHONTAS
## A DAUGHTER OF THE ALGONQUINS

These are difficult times. Our lives are in turmoil. Strange men from across the waters are settling on our land. Do they come in peace or do they come in war?

I am Pocahontas. I have a secret. I am afraid to tell my father. He is a great and mighty chief. He may not understand.

Should I tell my father? Should I risk his anger? On the other hand, if I don't tell him, things may get worse. I wish I knew what to do.

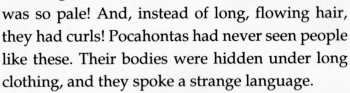

T WELVE-YEAR-OLD Pocahontas peered out through the dense forest. Ahead of her, in the clearing, stood a small group of strangers. For many minutes Pocahontas remained perfectly still, watching them. Their skin was so pale! And, instead of long, flowing hair, they had curls! Pocahontas had never seen people like these. Their bodies were hidden under long clothing, and they spoke a strange language.

"These must be the men my father warned me about," she thought to herself.

Pocahontas's father was Powhatan, the chief of Virginia's Algonquin Indians. In May 1607, he announced that some strange men had come from the sea in a huge winged canoe. No one could understand why they had come. No other white men lived in their land. This was the land of the Indians. The chief had warned his people to stay away from the newcomers.

Although Pocahontas knew of her father's warning, something about these strangers fascinated her. She wanted to find out more about them. She wondered, "Are they friendly or dangerous? What do these people really want?"

Pocahontas crept closer and closer to the clearing where the white men stood.

"I wish I could see their faces," she thought, filled with curiosity. "If I could look into their eyes, I would know if they were friend or foe."

Pocahontas, like other Indians, believed a person's true nature was visible in the eyes. She believed the eyes were the keys that unlocked the secrets to a person's soul. She waited anxiously, hoping someone would turn in her direction.

A twig snapped behind her. Fear flooded her body. Someone was following her. She remembered her father's words: "Do not go near the white men."

Another twig snapped. Pocahontas did not know what to do. Should she run? Should she scream for help? Should she try to hide?

Pocahontas felt a hand on her shoulder. In a panic, she whirled around and came face to face with a tall, yellow-haired man. She tried to run, but he grabbed her other shoulder.

"Slow down. I won't hurt you," he said softly.

Pocahontas could not understand the words he had spoken, but she saw that he had a gentle smile. And when she looked into his eyes, she knew he was a friend. His eyes were as blue as the sky. They sparkled with honesty and kindness.

"Why, you're just a little girl," the man said. "You must live in a nearby tribe."

Pocahontas shook her head in confusion. She had no idea what he was saying.

"My name is Captain John Smith," the man said, pointing to himself. Then he pointed at her. "What is your name?"

Pocahontas thought she knew what he was asking. "Pocahontas," she said shyly.

"Po-ca-hon-tas?" he asked haltingly.

She nodded. Then they smiled at each other. Even though they didn't speak the same language, they had communicated.

"Go home now," Captain Smith said, "and tell your people that we want to be friends. We mean you no harm."

Pocahontas did not understand the words, but she understood the message. She smiled, then ran off toward her village. When she got home, she went straight to her father to tell about her adventure.

FATHER, may I talk to you?" she asked as she entered his warm, dark wigwam. "I have something to tell you."

The aging Powhatan motioned for his daughter to approach him.

"Father," she began. She wanted to tell him about the white man she had met. She wanted to tell him that he shouldn't worry, that the white men were friendly. But she didn't know where to start.

She looked into her father's eyes. Then she remembered his warnings. Would he feel she had disobeyed him? What should she say to him?

She did not want to damage the trust he held for her. Never before had she gone against his rules.

Her excitement faded, and she quivered. "Oh, nothing really important," she murmured and quickly left his wigwam.

OVER the next few months, Pocahontas watched the tension between her people and the strangers increase. She feared a war would break out. This thought troubled her greatly. She knew they could live in peace if the groups would begin to communicate. How could she break down the barrier of mistrust between the peoples?

Her brother, Nantakas, noticed that Pocahontas was filled with sadness. One day he asked her, "What is wrong, Pocahontas? I do not see your smile anymore. You do not play joyfully as you once did."

"Oh, Nantakas," she sighed. "I wish I could tell you."

"You *can* tell me," he said softly. "I promise I will keep your secret."

Pocahontas looked at him. Of her many brothers, she loved him the most. She counted on him to help her decide what to do.

She told Nantakas about her meeting with Captain Smith. Nantakas whistled and gazed up at the sky.

"You were very lucky," he said. "You might have been killed or taken prisoner."

"But I wasn't!" cried Pocahontas. "The white man was nice to me. He would be nice to all of us, if only we gave him the chance. I think Father is wrong. He should not dislike the white men simply because they are different from us."

"Why don't you tell him that?" asked Nantakas.

Pocahontas sighed and stared at the clouds. "That's the problem," she said. "I'm not brave enough. I fear Father would be angry that I disobeyed him."

Nantakas patted Pocahontas on the shoulder. "Well," he said, "perhaps things will improve between our people and the white men anyway."

Pocahontas clung to that hope. But every day it grew dimmer. Every day Powhatan grumbled louder about the white settlers.

ONE day, in December 1607, Pocahontas was helping her mother grind corn when she heard shouts from the forest. Rushing outside, Pocahontas saw a dozen Algonquin warriors marching out of the woods. They were dragging a white man with them. Pocahontas stared. Her heart froze with panic. It was Captain John Smith.

"Nantakas!" Pocahontas cried, running over to her brother. "What happened?"

"Our braves found three white men on our hunting grounds," he told her. "The braves killed two of the men. This last one they have brought to Father as a prisoner."

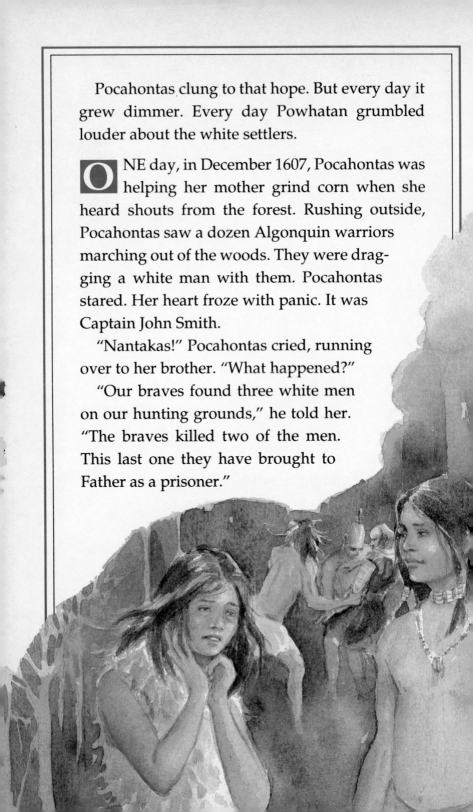

Pocahontas watched as the men led Captain Smith to the council house. She waited anxiously outside while her father and the other chiefs talked to him.

"This is terrible," Pocahontas whispered to Nantakas. "The prisoner is not an enemy. He is Captain Smith, the man I told you about. What do you think Father will do to him?"

Nantakas shrugged. "I don't know," he said. "But usually someone who trespasses on our hunting grounds is killed."

Pocahontas shuddered. Her heart ached when she thought of Captain Smith being killed.

"I should have said something," she chided herself. "I should have told Father how nice Captain Smith was to me."

At last the chiefs came out of the council house. With them came Captain Smith, his hands tied behind his back. Powhatan was the last to come out. When he stepped outside, he motioned to his warriors.

"Put this man to death," he ordered.

Horrified, Pocahontas tried to call out, but her voice caught in her throat. She felt dizzy and weak. The warriors led Captain Smith to a large boulder. They knocked him down and pushed his head onto the boulder.

Pocahontas clenched her hands. Her jaw tightened. Could she stand quietly and let the warriors kill Captain Smith? Or could she find some way to stop them?

AT that moment, Captain Smith looked directly at Pocahontas. When his piercing blue eyes met hers, she knew what she had to do.

Pocahontas rushed forward. She knelt down beside Captain Smith. "Stop!" she cried. "You must stop! Do not kill this man!"

Several warriors tried to pull her away. But she wrapped her arms tightly around Captain Smith's neck and placed her head against his. "If you kill him, you must first kill me!" she declared.

Powhatan motioned for the warriors to step back. Then he walked over to his young daughter. "What is the meaning of this?" he bellowed.

"Father, this man is a friend, not an enemy. Please promise to spare his life."

"I have given my orders."

"Father," Nantakas spoke up from the shadows. "What about the ancient laws? Can't any woman in the tribe claim one captive as her own?"

Powhatan hesitated. "Yes," he said at last. "But only if she offers her own life as a guarantee that this man will never harm our people."

"I do!" cried Pocahontas gratefully. "I offer my

life as a guarantee. If harm comes from this man, you can take my life."

Powhatan stared at his daughter. "Why are you taking this risk?" he asked.

"I can see in his eyes that he comes in friendship. I want us to be friends with the white man. Certainly friendship is better than war."

Powhatan shook his head. "You are brave and wise, my little one," he said. Then he turned to his warriors. "My daughter has claimed this man. Set him free."

Pocahontas's heart soared. She had found the courage to help bring the settlers and Indians closer to peace.

# ANNE BRADSTREET

## THE FIRST AMERICAN POET

We could no longer tolerate the conditions in England. Oh, yes! We had our home and friends. We had enough to eat. But people need more than that. They need to follow their personal beliefs. They need freedom to practice their own religion. Simon and I didn't have that in England.

So we came to America, full of hope. What a disappointment! Dirt! Squalor! Had we made a mistake?

ANNE and Simon Bradstreet huddled in the corner of a settler's shack in Salem, Massachusetts. It was their first night in this new land. They were far away from the comforts of England. During the day, they had learned of the hardships they would have to face here. They heard tales of terrible winters, sickness, and death. When Anne thought of the home they had left behind, tears filled her eyes.

"Tell me again, Simon," she whispered to her husband. "Help me remember why we are here."

"We are Puritans," Simon said softly. "And Puritans are not wanted in England. Remember how mean people were to us? Remember how we were hated? Here we don't have to worry about those things. Here we will be able to practice our religion freely."

"Yes," sighed Anne. "I remember now."

Simon recognized the fright and sadness in his wife's voice. "Perhaps we can try other settlements," Simon said. "Maybe things will look better somewhere else."

A few days later, Anne and Simon left Salem. They traveled twenty miles down the coast to the mouth of the Charles River. They settled in a tiny community called Charlestown. But life was no easier there. Charlestown settlers spent most of their time trying to tame the wilderness. They struggled to grow food in rocky, sandy soil. They faced long, frozen winters. The fear of disease was always with them.

Anne tried not to let the surroundings bother her. She busied herself with household chores. She cooked and cleaned. She made clothing and knit stockings. And, like all Puritan women, she attended church regularly.

Yet, Anne was not content with life in Charles-town. Her husband was very busy with the farm, the church, and his friends. Anne hadn't found it easy to make friends. She longed for someone with whom to share her feelings. She needed something to do to relieve her of the boredom of her daily routine.

One day Anne sat at a table with a piece of parchment and a quill pen. She began to write. She wrote about her husband, her home, and her feelings about the new land.

She found she loved writing. It gave her a freedom she had never before experienced.

The words that flowed from her heart erased the dreariness of her life. Her words took the form of poems.

Anne continued writing. She wrote about life and death. She wrote about the birth of her first baby. She wrote about neighbors and seasons and motherhood.

Anne kept all her poems hidden in a journal. She was afraid to let anyone know that she was writing poetry. She feared that this activity would not be approved by members of the Puritan community.

As time went on, she and Simon had a second baby, then a third, then a fourth. Eventually, they had eight children. They moved into a bigger house in a nearby town. Even with the responsibilities of eight children and a larger home, Anne still found the time to fulfill her need to write poetry. She also felt a growing need to share her poems with others.

ONE day Anne and her friends were visiting while mending clothes for the children. Anne gathered her courage and decided to share some of her favorite poems with her friends.

"I cannot believe you wrote these words," cried one friend in shock.

Anne was hurt by the reaction of her friend. "These poems express the feelings I've never been able to share with anyone. What is wrong with writing poetry?"

"Anne, you know perfectly well what is wrong with it. You are a woman. Women are not supposed to write poetry."

"That's right," added another friend. "Besides, we are Puritans. Puritans must be humble. We must be devoted to God. We cannot waste time writing poems. We should be doing God's work."

"These poems are not even about religion!" exclaimed a third woman. "They're all about you, Anne! It's wrong to spend so much time thinking of yourself."

Anne looked at her friends in dismay. "I thought you would understand," she said at last. "This is

the only way I have
to express myself. When
there is no one about, I can talk to
the paper. Writing poetry makes
me happy."

"It is not important whether you are
happy or not," replied the first woman. "It is important to do useful work. Writing these poems is
not a useful thing to do."

AFTER revealing her secret to her friends, Anne was filled with confusion. Was she so different from all the other Puritan women? Maybe her friends were right. Maybe she should not write poetry. For awhile she put away her parchment and quill pens. She stopped writing poems.

Anne busied herself with her chores as a Puritan wife and mother. But life without poetry seemed empty. She questioned whether she had made the right decision.

"What should I do?" she asked Simon in despair. "My life seems so empty without my poetry. My friends don't understand this part of me. I don't know what to do anymore."

"I cannot tell you what to do," he said gently. "You must make that decision for yourself." He took her hand and smiled at her. "But I can tell you this. Whatever you decide, I will support you. We have lived together for many years and you have always stood beside me. I will help you in every way I can."

Anne was grateful for Simon's attitude and support. Even though he hadn't given her an answer, he had given her a choice. Anne wanted to be like other people in the town. But she could not bear the thought of giving up something so important to her as a person. She spent long hours searching her heart.

"Simon, finally I have decided to continue my writing," she said.

"You know, Anne, that life will be different," Simon responded. "Those who we thought were our friends may abandon us. You may find yourself more alone than ever before. But rest assured that you will have the strength of your husband and children to count on."

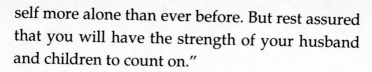

I N spite of Simon's warning, Anne was not prepared for the reaction to her decision to write. Her former friends became scornful and distant.

"You have no sense at all," hissed one woman.

"You have no respect for your religion!" cried another.

As word of Anne's decision spread, many townspeople turned against her. She was no longer welcome in certain homes. Some people ignored her. Others cursed her. One man even suggested that she leave town.

Although hurt, deep in her heart Anne knew that she had made the right decision. How could these people who had struggled so hard for their own freedom and independence deny it to another? How could she be offending her religion by expressing her innermost feelings? Wasn't that one of the reasons for coming to the new world?

"I came to America to find freedom," she told her husband and children. "And I have found it. I will follow my own heart. I will write poetry. I will say what I feel about myself and my life in this new world."

I N 1650, Anne used her freedom to take one final step. She sent her poems to a printer in England. There they were made into a book. The book was called *The Tenth Muse Lately Sprung Up in America*. When Anne read it, she had mixed feelings. She thought some of the poems were weak and rambling. But she found that people in England liked the book. They praised her poetry.

Life in America had often been difficult and disappointing. But by following her convictions and acting with courage, Anne felt she had discovered the true meaning of freedom. In the end, Anne triumphed. She—a woman—became America's first important poet.

# KING PHILIP

## An Indian Chief in Danger

I am Massasoit, powerful chief of the Wampanoags. Our tribe lives close to the new settlements of the white man.

One day, I took sixty braves with me and went to the village of Plymouth. We made a peace treaty with the white man.

The English people kept our treaty for forty years. They honored me by giving my little son an English name, Philip. One day, he would take my place as chief of the tribe.

THE American Indian chief, King Philip, stood at the top of Mount Hope near Bristol, Rhode Island. It was a beautiful, sunny day in 1675. Despite the weather, King Philip felt cold. A shiver of despair ran through his tall, dark frame. He glanced at the Wampanoag warriors standing near him. He knew they were awaiting his decision.

For many minutes King Philip did not speak. He simply stared at the homes of the English settlers in the valley below. This land once belonged to the Wampanoags. King Philip's father, Massasoit, had welcomed the English. He thought they would help keep out enemy tribes.

Now the English had taken over. Their homes sat on Wampanoag hunting grounds. Their leaders told the Indians what to do. Friends had become enemies.

Finally, King Philip let out a deep sigh. Then he turned to his warriors.

"Begin the attack," he said softly. Instantly the braves leaped for their weapons and ran down the hill. As they went, King Philip bowed his head in sorrow.

His braves attacked without mercy. They burned the homes, killed the settlers' cattle, destroyed their crops, and drove away their horses. They even broke the grinding stones that the settlers used in their mills. Any English who survived would face great hardship.

After the attack, Philip went to the hut of his uncle, Quadequina, an old and respected member of the tribe. As Philip walked through the door, his cousin saw his troubled face. She asked, "King Philip, what is wrong? What happened?"

"There is no turning back," Philip said to her. "I have just declared war on the settlers."

"There is no dishonor in declaring war," came the voice of Quadequina from deep within the hut.

Philip rushed in to embrace the old man. "I feel I've betrayed the memory of my father," he cried.

"Listen to me," said the old man sternly. "Your father, King Massasoit, was a faithful friend to the white settlers for forty years. That friendship led him to ask the governor to give you your English name. Since his death, I have watched you closely. I have seen you try to carry on his peaceful ways."

Quadequina, Massasoit's brother, paused a moment, then continued. "But times have changed. Today the white men do not act like friends. They continue to take our land. They drain our numbers. They convince many of our people to ignore our tradition and heritage. They want our people to adopt their strange ways and live with them in the settlement. They want our guns, our money, and our food. Soon we will have no life we can call our own."

Philip nodded and hugged the old man again. These were the words he needed to hear. They helped restore his courage and his confidence. He was reassured that he had made the right decision.

IN the beginning, the war went well for King Philip. Although he did not have as many men as the English, he had a unique strategy for fighting the white man. His Indians knew the woods well. They had hunted deer and birds in these forests. They were able to move rapidly and silently through the thick underbrush and muddy swamps. They could stage surprise attacks on the British troops, and, time after time, they won the day.

Sometimes Wampanoag warriors shot flaming arrows through the thatched roofs of settlers' cabins. In a matter of minutes, entire villages would be burned to the ground. At other times, they hid in the bushes waiting to ambush their enemy.

The settlers might sleep easily, thinking that the Indians were far away, only to awaken to an attack at dawn. Or the Indians might trick the settlers into an ambush in a ravine or swamp where there was no escape. The Indians carried muskets, as well as bows and arrows. They also had tomahawks for hand-to-hand fighting. Fear, too, was on their side.

After each attack, the Wampanoags slipped back into the forest, leaving no trace.

The British were no match for Philip's quick and cunning warriors. After all, the British militiamen were just the able-bodied men from each community. Few had ever fought before, and they carried muskets that were slow to reload. They had no training in how to fight Indians.

THE Indians' early successes pleased Philip. But these successes caused the British to change tactics. Philip heard the news from one of his scouts.

"The English soldiers have a new leader," the scout whispered to the braves. "His name is Benjamin Church. He used to be a friend to the Indians.

He knows our tactics well. He is using this knowledge against us. In the two days I have observed him, he has made many changes. He has thrown away the old-fashioned muskets. Now his men have new flintlocks. They are learning new ways to fight. Last night they split into small groups as soon as they left their camp."

As Philip listened, the muscles in his body began to tighten. It seemed that Church was adopting Indian methods. Such a move would wipe out Philip's advantage. The Wampanoags could never beat the English soldiers if they used the Indians' strategy. Philip said nothing to the scout, but a wave of despair washed over him.

IN the next few weeks, Philip's worst fears came to pass. The woods no longer belonged to his people. Church's soldiers turned up in the thickets, marshes, and bogs.

British soldiers were now ambushing Indians. They raided Wampanoag camps at night, driving Philip's people from their homes.

"I don't understand it," Philip lamented to Quadequina. "Church is striking our most protected camps. We are very well hidden. Yet he always knows where to look. How can this be?"

"The most dangerous enemy is the one who used to be a friend," said Quadequina slowly.

"What are you suggesting?" quizzed Philip. "Do you think our own people are betraying us?"

Quadequina did not answer, but merely looked at Philip with his clear dark eyes. Philip felt an arrow of fear pierce his heart.

After leaving Quadequina, Philip called for his most trusted scouts. He needed desperately to know if his uncle was right. Could any of his own men have betrayed him? Could a Wampanoag warrior be working for Church? He hoped it wasn't true. But he had to be certain.

The scout brought his answer. A number of Wampanoag warriors had been taken prisoner and were now working for the enemy.

"Why would they betray us?" wailed Philip.

"Church treats his Indian prisoners well," responded the scout. "He gives them plenty of food and a decent place to live. In this way, he wins their friendship. They in turn agree to act as his guides. They are leading him straight to our hiding places."

Philip stood quietly among the trees. He was furious with the traitors. His thoughts were interrupted by a messenger.

"Church has attacked our main campground!" the messenger cried breathlessly.

"When did this happen?" demanded Philip.

"Last night, during the snowstorm. The soldiers came out of nowhere. They killed almost a thousand of our people. They even killed Quadequina."

A terrible sense of loss filled the heart of King Philip. He grieved for his dear friend and his brave warriors. It was the final blow. The battle was lost. With so many warriors dead, Philip had no chance left. And without Quadequina, he had no one to turn to for strength.

In his heart, Philip gave up all hope on that bitter December night. But for the honor of his people, he kept fighting. By the following summer, his army was almost gone. In August of 1676, he headed back to Mount Hope to meet with the few warriors still on his side.

But even here, Philip was betrayed. A Wampanoag warrior slipped out of camp and ran to join Benjamin Church. He told Church where to find Philip.

SOON Church's troops invaded Mount Hope. Over half of them were Indians who had joined the English side. They crept up on the sleeping Wampanoags during the night and surrounded the camp. King Philip and his warriors tried to escape to the swamp, but were trapped.

The Indian who had betrayed Philip took the first shot. That one shot ended the hopes of the Wampanoags. With Philip, their brave leader, gone, the fight was over. The Indian way of life would be changed forever.

# John Peter Zenger

## Freedom of the Press

I never thought I would have a publisher as a prison mate! Peter Zenger is in the next cell. He's an educated man, not a common thief like I am. What could he have done? They say he published a newspaper that made the governor mad.

This Zenger must really believe in his principles. Spending time in jail just to say something! It doesn't make sense to me.

J OHN Peter Zenger, you are under arrest." The sheriff spoke harshly, flashing his badge in John's face. "You must come with me."

"What are you talking about?" John cried. He stood up from his desk in the newspaper printing office that he owned. "Who has ordered my arrest?"

"William Cosby, the Royal Governor of New York," answered the sheriff.

"And what are the charges?" demanded John.

"Your newspaper, the *New York Weekly Journal,* has printed articles attacking the Governor."

"And is that a crime?" shouted John.

"Yes," said the sheriff stiffly. "The Governor has decided that it is."

John Peter Zenger sighed. He should have expected this. For months Governor Cosby had been trying to close down the *Journal* because he did not like to read articles criticizing his rule. After all, Cosby had been appointed by the King of England. Twice the Governor had tried to get a grand jury to bring charges against Zenger. Both times the grand jury had refused. Now, in November 1734, Cosby was taking a new approach. He was charging Zenger with libel. He accused Zenger of printing statements that hurt the Governor's reputation.

Zenger followed the sheriff out of the printing office. It was a Sunday afternoon. Crowds of people strolled through the streets of New York City. They watched, shocked, as the sheriff led Zenger in handcuffs to City Hall. At City Hall, the sheriff took him to the third floor and locked him in a cell.

ZENGER sat glumly on the floor of the cell. He was surrounded by drunks and petty thieves. The air was cold and stale. Zenger hoped his wife Anna would arrive soon. If she could pay his bail, he would be free until the trial. But hours passed. No one came. Finally, he called to the jailer.

"Please, sir, can you tell me if my wife has arrived?"

"You're Zenger, right?" asked the jailer.

"Yes," said Zenger, his spirits rising. "I'm John Peter Zenger."

"Well, you are not allowed to see your wife. Or anyone else, for that matter. Governor's orders."

"But what about bail?" asked Zenger anxiously.

"You'll never make bail," said the jailer flatly. "It's been set at 400 pounds."

"No!" cried John. "That's impossible! Why that's ten times more than my life savings!"

"You'll just have to stay in jail then if you can't pay your bail," said the jailer.

The man started to walk away. But suddenly he turned on his heel and looked back at Zenger. "What did you do to make the Governor so angry?" asked the jailer.

"I publish a newspaper that prints the truth," Zenger replied bitterly.

"Yeah?" the jailer took a step closer. "And what's the truth?"

"The truth is that Governor Cosby is greedy and corrupt. Were you aware that he once had a farmer whipped because the man's wagon got in his way?

Did you know that he accepted a bribe of 1,000 pounds from city assemblymen? Were you aware that he unfairly fixed the last two elections in this city? He even removed judges from office so he could appoint new ones that he liked!"

Zenger's face flushed with anger as he described the Governor's behind-the-scenes activities. The jailer listened in silence. Finally he shook his head.

"No," he said, "I didn't know all that. Maybe next week I'll buy a copy of your paper."

The next week, however, no copy of the *Journal* appeared. John Peter Zenger could not print it. He was still in jail.

INALLY, the guards allowed Anna Zenger and her two sons to see Zenger. The prisoner was overjoyed. After visiting, he explained how important it was for them to continue his work.

"You must keep the newspaper running. Print all the articles my writers give you," he whispered. "And sign them all 'Anonymous.' That way Governor Cosby won't know who wrote them. He won't be able to punish more writers."

Anna Zenger and her sons listened carefully. They followed all of Zenger's instructions. And the next week, they managed to print the *Journal*. Over the next eight months, while Zenger remained in jail, they never missed a single issue.

Zenger's friends tried to help him. Several of them were lawyers and offered to defend him. But Governor Cosby acted quickly. He took away their licenses so they could no longer practice law.

Zenger's friends did not give up. Secretly, they went to Pennsylvania and talked to the elderly lawyer Andrew Hamilton, the best legal mind in America. They asked him to help Zenger.

Meanwhile, the court appointed a lawyer to defend Zenger. This new lawyer, John Chambers, was young and inexperienced. Worse, he supported the policies of Governor Cosby.

THE trial finally began on August 4, 1735. Chambers made only a few mild comments. While his lawyer spoke, Zenger's hopes for winning the case faded. It was clear Chambers believed that Zenger would be found guilty. Everyone else in the courtroom thought the same thing. When the jury got up to leave the room, Zenger knew the case was lost. He slumped in his chair and buried his face in his hands.

Then, all of a sudden, a man called out from the back of the courtroom.

"If it please the court," said the elderly gentleman, "I wish to defend Mr. Zenger."

The people in the courtroom turned to stare at the man. Silence fell over the room as people began to recognize him. He was Andrew Hamilton, the famous lawyer from Philadelphia. But no one could believe he was here. Why would he want to defend John Peter Zenger against the mighty Governor of New York? They knew the Governor would be furious.

Hamilton was not supposed to take new cases because of his health. Yet it was true. He was here to take this case because he believed in the cause of freedom of the press. He wanted to defend this principle in a court of law.

Slowly Hamilton approached the jury. "My defense is simple," he said. "John Peter Zenger printed no lies. Every word that has appeared in his newspaper is true. The current libel law violates the freedom we sought to gain when we came to this country. Libel can occur only when *false* statements are printed. People who print lies should be thrown in jail. But no one should be jailed for printing the truth."

As Hamilton spoke, the members of the jury sat motionless. They listened to his clear, strong voice. His words made sense to them. They began to look at the case in a new light.

"This case is not just about the fate of one poor printer," Hamilton concluded. "It affects every free person in America. It will decide whether people in our land have the right to speak and print the truth. Yes, John Peter Zenger's cause is an important cause. It is the best cause. It is the cause of liberty. You must find my client not guilty."

Hamilton bowed to the jury. Then he took his place beside Zenger.

T HE jury took only ten minutes to reach a verdict. The judge called for the jury's decision.

"Not guilty," stated the leader of the jury.

Zenger shook Hamilton's hand gratefully.

"Do not thank me," the great lawyer said. "I came here to defend you because your case is tied to the fate of every man, woman, and child in this country. And to future generations. But I am happy for you—and for our country. Liberty has triumphed. Now every citizen can enjoy true freedom—freedom of speech and freedom of the press."

THE NEW WORLD

Places in *Risking It All*

(CANADA)

Hudson Bay

NORTH

AMERICA

(UNITED STATES)

SEE INSET MAP BELOW

ATLANTIC OCEAN

PACIFIC OCEAN

SOUTH

(BRAZIL)

AMERICA

New Hampshire

Massachusetts

New York

Rhode Island

Connecticut

Pennsylvania

New Jersey

Delaware

Maryland

Virginia

North Carolina

South Carolina

Georgia

N